A BANK STREET MUSEUM BOOK

PLANETARIUM

By Barbara Brenner • Illustrated by Ron Miller

With an introduction by Dr. William R. Alschuler, Science Consultant

A Byron Preiss Book

BANTAM BOOKS
NEW YORK • TORONTO • LONDON • SYDNEY • AUCKLAND

To Carl, in memory of stargazing.
–B.B.

PLANETARIUM
A Bantam Book/March 1993

Series graphic design by Alex Jay/Studio J
Senior Editor: Sarah Feldman
Assistant Editor: Kathy Huck
Special thanks to Betsy Gould, William H. Hooks, Hope Innelli,
James A. Levine, and Howard Zimmerman.
Additional scientific review from Suzanne Gurton,
Astronomical Writer and Producer, Hayden Planetarium.

Library of Congress Cataloging-in-Publication Data

Brenner, Barbara.
Planetarium/Barbara Brenner;
illustrated by Ron Miller.
p. cm — (Bank Street museum book)
"A Byron Preiss book."
Summary: Presents facts about each planet through
a tour of a planetarium.
ISBN 0-553-07619-1. — ISBN 0-553-35428-0 (pbk.)
1. Planeteria — Juvenile literature. [1. Outer Space.]
I. Miller, Ron, 1947-   . II. Title.   III. Series.
QB70.B74   1992
520'.74 — dc20
91-6629
CIP
AC

Published simultaneously in the United States and Canada

Bantam Books are published by Bantam Books, a division of Bantam Doubleday Dell
Publishing Group, Inc. Its trademark, consisting of the words "Bantam Books" and the
portrayal of a rooster, is Registered in U.S. Patent and Trademark Office and in other
countries. Marca Registrada. Bantam Books, 666 Fifth Avenue, New York, New York 10103.

PRINTED IN THE UNITED STATES OF AMERICA
0 9 8 7 6 5 4 3 2 1

Introduction

All through my years in grade school, the principal of my school used to come around once a year and give a talk about the planets and the Sun, and how we were going to travel to them on giant spaceships. I later found out that most parents, including my own, thought he was a bit crazy for talking about rockets to the moon and Earth satellites. This was in the early 1950s when many people considered such things science fiction. Yet just a few years later, in 1957, the first satellites went up. My principal inspired me to look to the skies to dream of interplanetary voyages, and to set my sights on becoming an astronomer.

Today we have actually begun these great voyages and can now sit at home and watch wonderful live TV pictures showing close-ups of sulphur volcanoes and ice seas on the moons of Jupiter, Uranus spinning like a knocked-over top, and the patterns of fierce cold winds of Neptune. Still, I get a great thrill any time I go outside on a dark, clear night, far from city lights, and look up at all the stars, and let my eye wander along the Milky Way. If you live in a big city, then just cast your eye upon the Moon. Binoculars or a very small telescope (on a steady mount) will reveal amazing details of mountains, cliffs, craters, and dusty plains. This book should send you on your way to space. Use it, and look at the sky with new questions and new dreams!

Dr. William R. Alschuler
President, Future Museums

If the Sun
were an orange,
Mercury would be
a grain of sand.
Venus,
a pinhead.
Earth,
another pinhead.
Mars, a grain of sand.
Jupiter,
a marble.
Saturn,
a pea.
Uranus,
a small pill.
Neptune,
a pill.
Pluto,
a third pinhead.
　　—A. E. Nourse

If you flew in a spaceship at 5,000 miles per hour
through the center of the solar system starting at
the Sun, it would take eighty-four years to get
past Pluto.

Welcome to the Planetarium.
You are about to take a trip
through our solar system. But
first climb aboard *Fantasy 1*
and let's see where we are...

CONTENTS

We're in the Planetarium…in a city…
in the United States…on Earth…

Earth is part of our solar system...
in a galaxy....

There are billions of galaxies in
the universe.

Now let's get another view
of where we're going.

Pluto

Neptune

Uranus

Saturn

THE SOLAR SYSTEM

You're looking at our solar system. There's Earth – the third planet out from the Sun. It's called a *solar* system because all the planets revolve around a sun. Solar means having to do with a sun.

Up to now we have discovered nine planets, fifty-seven moons, several dozen comets, several million asteroids, and billions of meteorites in our solar system.

The nine planets (in order from the Sun) are Mercury, Venus, Earth, Mars, Jupiter, Saturn, Uranus, Neptune, Pluto.

Earth

Mercury

Mars

Venus

Jupiter

They look like a bunch of spinning balls revolving around a central spinning ball.

That's because the planets are rotating (spinning on their axes), and also revolving around the Sun.

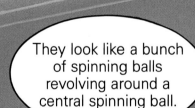

A solar system is a group of planets in orbit around a sun, all held together by gravity. A galaxy is a huge system of stars, gas, and dust in orbit around a central point.

Here's a good device to help you remember the planets. My *(Mercury)* Very *(Venus)* Excited *(Earth)* Mother *(Mars)* Just *(Jupiter)* Served *(Saturn)* Us *(Uranus)* Nine *(Neptune)* Pizzas *(Pluto)*.

Why don't the planets all fly away from each other?

Because of gravity.

THIS WAY TO THE HALL OF GRAVITY
→

HALL OF GRAVITY

You can't see it or feel it, but this hall is full of gravity! Gravity is everywhere in the universe. You can feel the pull of gravity every time you lift something. If there were no gravity you couldn't stay seated in a chair or pour a glass of water. Gravity is a mysterious force. No one knows exactly how it works, but here's what it does.

Earth's gravity pulls everything toward the center of the Earth. That's what keeps us on its surface. The more mass an object has, the stronger its pull of gravity. Earth has more mass than the Moon, so its gravity is stronger than the Moon's. You would weigh less on the Moon than on Earth because the Moon has a weaker pull of gravity. That's why the astronauts were able to walk lightly there even in heavy spacesuits.

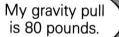

My gravity pull is 80 pounds.

Experiment 1
When you weigh yourself, you're really measuring how much gravity pulls on you.

Experiment 2
This robot has a pail with a foam ball inside. The robot turns the pail upside down. What happens? *The ball falls out of the pail.*

Now the robot picks up the string and whirls the pail around its head. What happens? *The ball stays in the pail.*

Gravity is pulling the ball toward the ground. At the same time, the force of the whirling motion is balancing the force of gravity, so the ball stays in the pail.

Suppose the robot were to swing the pail just a little. That force might not be enough to balance gravity's pull.

Gravity is what keeps our solar system together. The Earth stays in its path around the Sun because of gravity. The Moon travels around Earth because of gravity. Even Neptune, one of the farthest planets in our system, feels the pull of the Sun's gravity.

The farther away two objects are from each other, the weaker the pull between them. That's why Pluto, the farthest planet from the Sun, is held so weakly by the Sun and travels around its orbit so slowly.

It's a tie every time.

Every physical body has mass, whether it's a rock or a feather. Mass is a measure of the amount of material in the object.
Weight is a measurement of how much gravity pulls on an object's mass.

We could try these experiments at home.

THIS WAY TO THE SUN ROOM (Don't forget your sungoggles.)
→

Experiment 3
This robot has two balls. One weighs 2 pounds. One weighs half a pound. The robot drops both balls at the same time. Which ball hits the floor first? *They hit the ground at the same time.* The pull of Earth's gravity on a falling object makes it fall at the same rate, whether the object is light or heavy.

SUN ROOM

Welcome to the Sun! This model shows you what it would be like if you could get close to the Sun. Actually, the Sun is about 93 million miles away from Earth. And it's a good thing, too. That "big orange" is hot – about 10,000 degrees F on its outside surface! If the Earth were closer to the Sun, we wouldn't be here. All our water would evaporate. Nothing could live.

The Sun is a star. Like other stars, it revolves slowly around the center of the Milky Way, our galaxy. The Sun also rotates (spins) on its axis. But it doesn't "rise" and "set" every day. It just *looks* that way to us. What's really happening is that Earth is rotating on its own axis while it is moving around the Sun. In fact, the planets, satellites, asteroids, and comets all move in orbit around the Sun. The Sun's gravity holds everything in place.

So when we see the Sun moving across the sky, it's because the Earth is moving—even though we don't feel it!

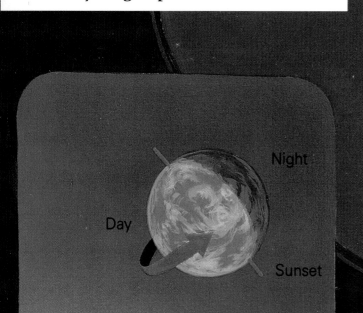

Night

Day

Sunset

It takes 24 hours for the Earth to complete one rotation on its axis. We call this period of time one day.

It takes about 365 days for the Earth to complete one revolution around the Sun. We call this period of time one year.

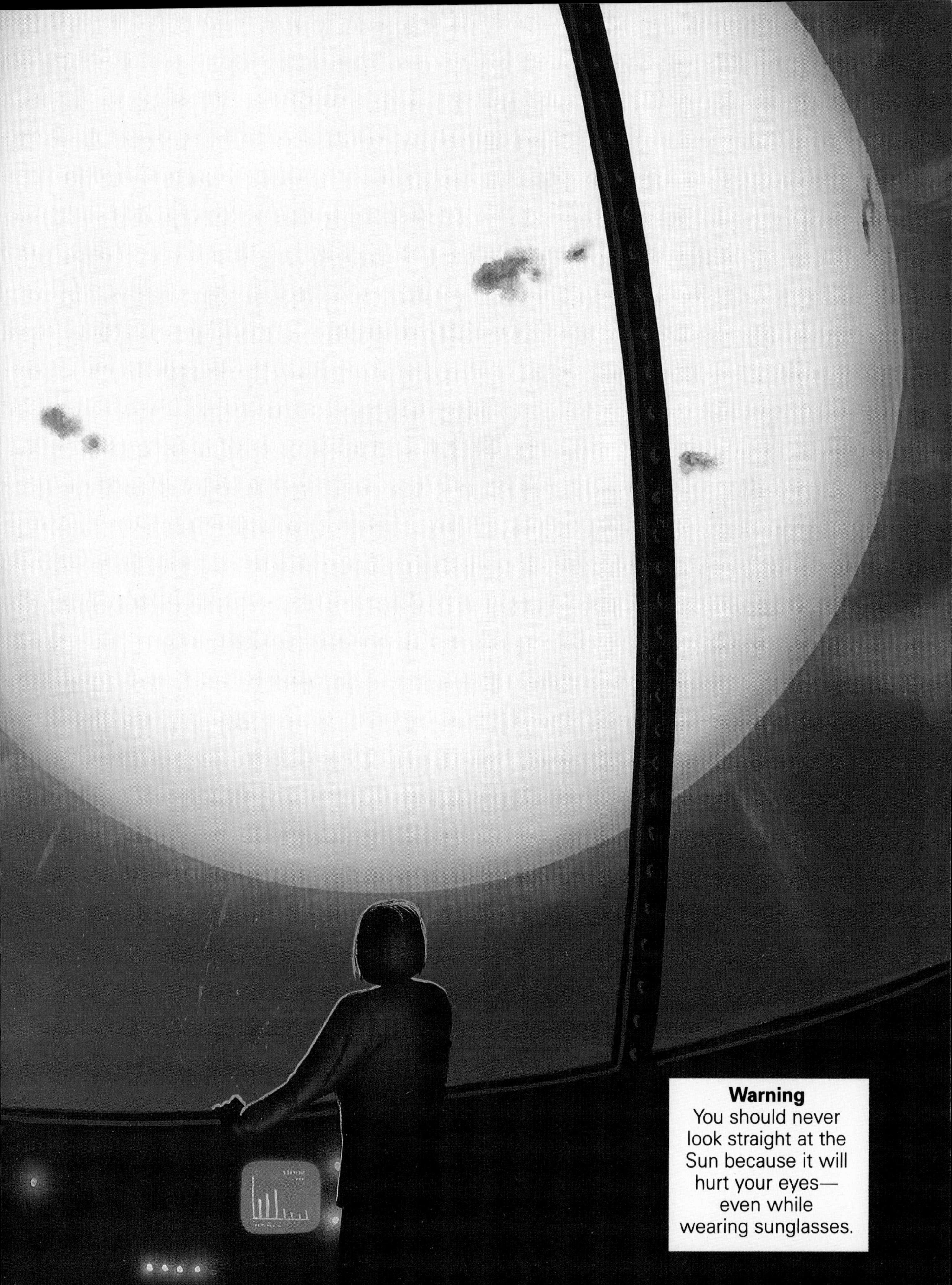

Warning
You should never look straight at the Sun because it will hurt your eyes—even while wearing sunglasses.

The Sun is one of the smaller stars. But it is giant compared to the planets in our solar system. If the Sun were hollow, more than a million Earths could fit inside it.

The most important thing about the Sun is its making of energy. This comes from the core – that white-hot part in the center. In the core, giant nuclear explosions take place all the time. They are fueled by hydrogen gases and, like hydrogen bombs, they release enormous quantities of energy. This energy is constantly working its way to the surface of the Sun. The Sun uses up over 4 million tons of hydrogen per second. But it still has enough hydrogen to last for the next 5 billion years.

Core

Photosphere

Wow! If only scientists could harness the Sun's power!

I've seen lights and toys that run on solar energy.

Experiment
Take two large cans. Paint one black. Fill both with cold water. Put them both out in the sun on a sunny day.

After two hours, measure the temperature of the water in each can. Which can of water is warmer? Which one collected more solar energy? *It is the black one, because the color black absorbs more light than any other color.*

How could you use this idea in your own home?

The outer layer of the Sun, the photosphere, is made up of boiling gases. That's why the Sun looks to us like a ball of fire.

The Sun revolves around our galaxy. It completes one orbit every 225 million years.

Sunspots

Sunspots are giant storms on the surface of the Sun. One of these "spots" can release enough electrical energy to take care of all Earth's energy for 1 million years. Sunspots come in cycles. Maximum numbers of sunspots appear about every 22 years. The last big year for sunspots was 1991. So the next one will be 2013.

The largest sunspot ever seen was recorded on April 18, 1947. It covered an area of 7 billion square miles.

Going toward Earth in a spaceship you might see the Sun this way at the edge of Earth's horizon.

Northern Lights

If the energy in a sunspot is released in an explosion, particles of matter are sent sailing into space. They can collide with our atmosphere and can form a curtain of light – the "northern lights" or aurora borealis. (On the other side of the equator it is the "southern lights" or aurora australis.)

The Sun is certainly impressive. No wonder ancient people worshiped it and built temples to it. They sensed that the Sun is the source of all life. Without the Sun's energy, there would be no plants. If there were no plants, there would be no animals. Without the Sun, Earth would be a cold, dark, lifeless desert.

Sun Facts

Average distance from Earth:
93,000,000 miles

Diameter at equator:
864,000 miles

Surface temperature:
10,000 degrees F

Completes one rotation on its axis in:
25 days at its equator
35 days at its poles

A person who weighs 100 pounds on Earth would weigh 2,800 pounds on the Sun.

THIS WAY TO THE HALL OF MERCURY
→

HALL OF MERCURY

You're looking at the dividing line between day and night on the rocky desert that is the planet Mercury.

Mercury is the planet closest to the Sun. Mercury gets a heavy dose of solar heat, which long ago boiled away any water or atmosphere that it may have had. Temperatures get up to 800 degrees F during a Mercury day. During the long nights, it can get down to -350 degrees F. Mercury has the greatest differences in temperature of any planet in our solar system.

The Sun's gravity really pulls little Mercury. Mercury revolves around the Sun much faster than Earth – one revolution in about 88 Earth days.

The craters you can see were probably made by meteors. At some time in the past, a huge rock slammed into Mercury and broke through its crust. The lava from its core leaked out and welled up. When it cooked, its waves hardened into rock and formed the Caloris basin. The Caloris basin is about 860 miles wide.

Mercury Facts

The diameter of Mercury is slightly more than one-third that of Earth.

Position from Sun: Number 1

Average distance from Sun: 36,000,000 miles

Diameter at equator: 3,050 miles

Mercury year: 88 Earth days

A Mercury day is: 59 Earth days

If you weigh 100 pounds on Earth, you would weigh 38 pounds on Mercury.

Satellites: None known

Mercury Watch

This planet is hard to spot due to the Sun's glare. It is possible to see it when it's farthest from the Sun's direction in the sky. Look for it just after sunset or just before sunrise.

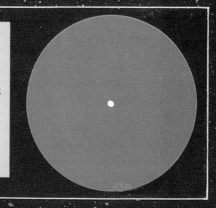

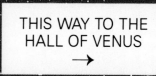

THIS WAY TO THE HALL OF VENUS
→

Venus Facts

The diameter of Venus is almost the same as that of Earth.

Position from Sun:
Number 2

Average distance from Sun:
67,000,000 miles

Diameter at equator:
7,520 miles

Venus year:
225 Earth days

A Venus day is:
243 Earth days

If you weigh 100 pounds on Earth, you would weigh 91 pounds on Venus.

Satellites:
None known

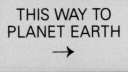

THIS WAY TO
PLANET EARTH
→

HALL OF VENUS
WEIRD AND DEADLY

We are now looking at the surface of Venus. Venus is named after the Greek goddess of love. But in reality, Venus is not lovely. It is surrounded by deadly carbon dioxide. Its clouds are sulfuric acid instead of water vapor. It's too hot for anyone from Earth to live there, and even if you could stand the heat, you'd be crushed by the air pressure, which would be as great as if you were diving 3,000 feet into the ocean. Venus is also contrary. It rotates on its axis opposite to the rotation direction of every other planet. If there were people on Venus, they would see the Sun rise in the west and set in the east.

In 1975, the first successful space probe to Venus began to send back information. Before that time, space probes were crushed by the heavy atmosphere before they could send any data. So far, twenty-one spacecraft have visited Venus. None has ever returned. The latest, *Magellan,* is now making detailed maps of Venus.

Venus is almost the same size as Earth, but its mountain ranges are much higher. They may be the largest ranges of mountains in our solar system.

Venus Watch
Look for Venus in the sky just after sunset or just before sunrise. It shines very brightly because its 20-mile-thick cloud cover reflects sunlight like a field of snow.

PLANET EARTH

Our next stop is planet Earth....Here you're seeing the view of Earth that the astronauts got from *Apollo 17* in 1972.

From out here Earth looks like a big blue-and-white ball. The blue is water, which covers 71 percent of Earth. The white is ice at the north and south poles and swirling clouds. If you look hard, you can see the shapes of the continents. Can you find the United States?

The Earth's *crust* is a thin skin of rock about 22 miles thick. It's made of granite and other lightweight rocks. Under the crust is the *mantle,* a deep, hot layer of basalt rock nearly 1,800 miles thick. Then comes the *core.* The outer core is molten metal. The inner *core* may be iron and nickel.

Earth is the only planet in our solar system known to have life. Our distance from the Sun has something to do with it. Not too near. Not too far. We have seasons because the Earth's axis tips toward the Sun for a while and then away from it for a while as the Earth spins. The part of Earth that is toward the Sun each day has summer. The part that's tilted away from the Sun has winter.

One of the things that keeps us going is Earth's atmosphere. It lies over us like a blanket, and it's held in place by the force of gravity. The atmosphere provides the air we breathe. It is a shield against the Sun's dangerous rays. It holds in the Sun's heat. The ozone layer is part of this protection.

I read that pollution has already caused a hole in the ozone layer of the atmosphere.

A lot of the pollution comes from cars.

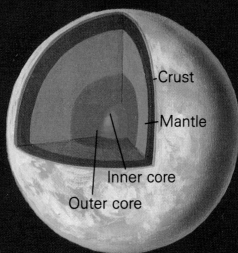

Crust

Mantle

Inner core

Outer core

Earth Facts

Position from Sun:
Number 3

Average distance
from Sun:
93,000,000 miles

Diameter at equator:
7,930 miles

Orbits Sun in:
1 year

An Earth day is:
23 hours, 56 minutes,
4 seconds

Satellites:
1 Moon

Surface area covered
by ocean:
71 percent

Earth Myths

In the seventeenth century, Dr.
Edmund Halley believed that the
Earth was hollow under a 500-mile-
thick crust and had three planets
inside it!

In the eighteenth century, Leonard
Euler said that people lived inside
the Earth and that it had its own sun.

In the nineteenth century, Captain
John Cleves Symmes thought that
you could reach the center of Earth
through large holes in the north
and south poles.

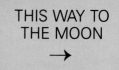

THIS WAY TO
THE MOON
→

THE MOON

Now *Fantasy 1* has landed on the surface of our Moon model.

The Moon is our space partner – our natural satellite. A satellite is an object that orbits a planet. Some planets have more than one moon.

From Earth, the Moon looks bright, but its light is actually reflected sunlight. If the Moon didn't reflect the Sun's light, it would be so dim that we might not see it at all!

The Moon has no atmosphere, no air, and no water. So it has no clouds, no wind, and no rain. It's either very hot or very cold depending on how it's turned in relation to the Sun. We could live on the Moon *only* if we constructed an enclosed environment, such as an airtight building.

The Moon's gravity causes tides in Earth's oceans. When the Moon is overhead, its gravitational pull causes the water directly below it and on the other side of the Earth to swell. At those places it will be high tide.

The Moon's sky is always black, because the Moon has no atmosphere.

The dark areas seen on the surface of the moon are called *maria*. They are basins that may have been formed by huge meteorites. Later they were filled by lava. *Maria* is the Latin name for seas. Ancient astronomers thought the big dark areas on the Moon were oceans.

There are mountain ranges on the Moon that rise as high as 25,000 feet, higher than Mount McKinley in Alaska.

Moon Theories

1. The Moon is a piece broken off from Earth.
2. Earth collided with another planet during the time when Earth's crust was forming. Material from Earth squirted out and stuck to particles from the other planet. So the Moon is a piece of Earth welded together with a piece of an unknown planet.
3. The Earth and the Moon formed at the same time, but separately.

Moon Facts

The diameter of the Moon is one-quarter that of Earth.

Position from Sun: Orbits Earth, third planet from Sun

Average distance from Earth: 240,000 miles

Diameter at equator: 2,170 miles

A Moon day is: 27.3 Earth days

Phases repeat every: 29.5 days

A person who weighs 100 pounds on Earth would weigh 17 pounds on the Moon.

The oldest rocks on the Moon have been dated at 4.4 billion years. These rocks, collected by spacecraft and by astronauts, help scientists to figure out how the Moon and the Earth may have been formed.

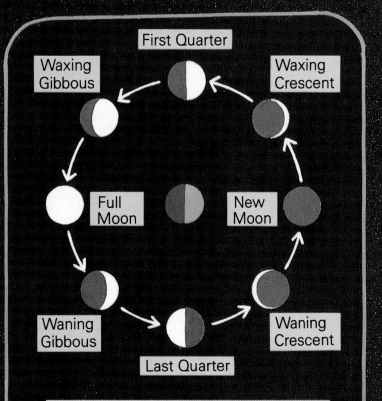

First Quarter

Waxing Gibbous

Waxing Crescent

Full Moon

New Moon

Waning Gibbous

Waning Crescent

Last Quarter

Phases of the Moon
It takes the Moon slightly less than a month—29 days, 12 hours, 44 minutes, 2.78 seconds—to orbit our planet. As the Moon travels around the Earth, we see different amounts of the lighted part. These changing shapes are called *phases*.

MOON EXPLORERS

The Moon is the only surface in space that people have landed on. Since there's no atmosphere on the Moon, nothing changes on the surface. The footprints that the astronauts left will probably be there for ages to come.

Apollo 11 landed the first two astronauts on the Moon (1969, United States). They brought back rock samples.

Luna 2 was the first spacecraft to hit the Moon (1959, Soviet Union).

Ranger 7 sent back over 4,000 pictures of the Moon (1964, United States).

Five Surveyor spacecraft landed on the Moon (1966-68, United States).

Luna 16 landed on the Moon and brought back lunar soil (1970, Soviet Union).

The astronauts were the first people to see the far side of the Moon.

They saw it from orbit but didn't walk there.

Moon Fact
The Moon seems to be moving away from Earth at a rate of about 1 inch a year.

THIS WAY TO THE HALL OF MARS
→

HALL OF MARS
THE RED PLANET

If we were 14,000 miles from Mars in *Mariner 9*, it would look like this. Mars is the planet next door to Earth, and at its closest it is 50 million miles away from us. It looks red because it is covered by a layer of soft red iron oxide – sandlike rust. When the winds blow and raise dust from the surface they make the sky around Mars look pink.

Mars is the planet most like Earth. But it's only half as big and it has very little air or water. Its seasons are much more extreme than on Earth. Winter on Mars can have temperatures of -200 degrees F!

The largest volcano we know of in the solar system is on Mars. It's called Olympus Mons. It's 15 miles high, about six times the height of Hawaii's Mauna Loa.

The most interesting feature of Mars is its channels, which were discovered in 1869. Some people thought they might have been canals created by some kind of intelligent life, but they're probably ancient channels formed when Mars was warmer and had flowing water.

We used to think there might be life on Mars. *Mariner 9* took pictures of it in 1971, and *Viking 1* and *Viking 2* visited it in 1976. In fact, more spacecraft have successfully explored Mars than any other planet. They have seen no evidence of life there – so far.

Mars has two moons, Phobos and Deimos. They're shaped like potatoes, and they're tiny. Phobos is about 13 miles long. Deimos is 9 miles long. *Deimos* means demon, *Phobos* means fear.

Which of the following would you need to establish a Martian space colony?

1. Water
2. Air
3. Warm clothes
4. Weighted shoes
5. Sunglasses
6. A new calendar

Phobos

The first person to see Mars through a telescope was Galileo.

Mars Facts

The diameter of Mars is one-half that of Earth.

Position from Sun: Number 4

Average distance from Sun: 142,000,000 miles

Diameter at equator: 4,220 miles

A Mars year is: 687 Earth days

A Mars day is: 24 hours, 37 minutes

If you weigh 100 pounds on Earth, you would weigh 38 pounds on Mars.

Satellites: 2

Mars Watch

You can often find Mars in the sky. It has a red cast even from Earth. That's why it's called the Red Planet.

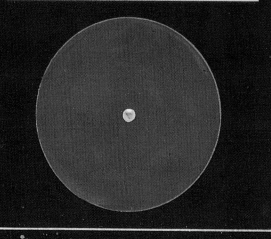

Deimos

THIS WAY TO THE HALL OF JUPITER
→

HALL OF JUPITER
THE GIANT

You are now in a specially designed space pod swinging around the planet Jupiter. Jupiter is a giant – bigger than all the other planets put together.

This is the view that *Voyager 1* and *Voyager 2* had of Jupiter in 1979. Jupiter looks like a big round ball circled by bands of color. The dark bands are called *belts*. The light ones are called *zones*. They are moving swirls of gases that make up part of its surface. As the gases get closer to the core of Jupiter, they get thicker. Jupiter may have a solid core, but scientists are fairly certain that most of Jupiter is made up of hydrogen, helium, ammonia, and methane in gas or liquid form.

Can you see an area that might be called the Great Red Spot? The Great Red Spot is really a storm on Jupiter's surface, and it's about 25,000 miles long, or about the size of three Earths. Scientists have been watching this storm for about 400 years. It doesn't go away.

I see the Great Red Spot over there, where the seven would be on a clock.

Jupiter has at least sixteen moons. The biggest are Io, Europa, Ganymede, and Callisto. They were discovered by Galileo and the German astronomer Marius almost at the same time, in 1610.

Recently it was discovered that Jupiter has rings. They're very faint and about 80,000 miles from the planet itself. They're made of fine particles that gleam like dust specks in a beam of light.

Jupiter Watch
Jupiter will appear in the night sky as a very bright "star" that doesn't twinkle. Check your newspaper for the times and positions.

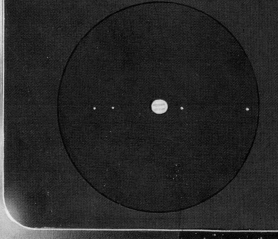

Jupiter Facts

The diameter of Jupiter is 11.2 times greater than that of Earth.

Position from Sun: Number 5

Average distance from Sun: 484,000,000 miles

Diameter at equator: 89,000 miles

A Jupiter year is: 11.9 Earth years

A Jupiter day is: 9 hours, 53 minutes

A person who weighs 100 pounds on Earth would weigh 234 pounds on Jupiter.

Satellites: 16 known moons Rings

THIS WAY TO THE HALL OF SATURN
→

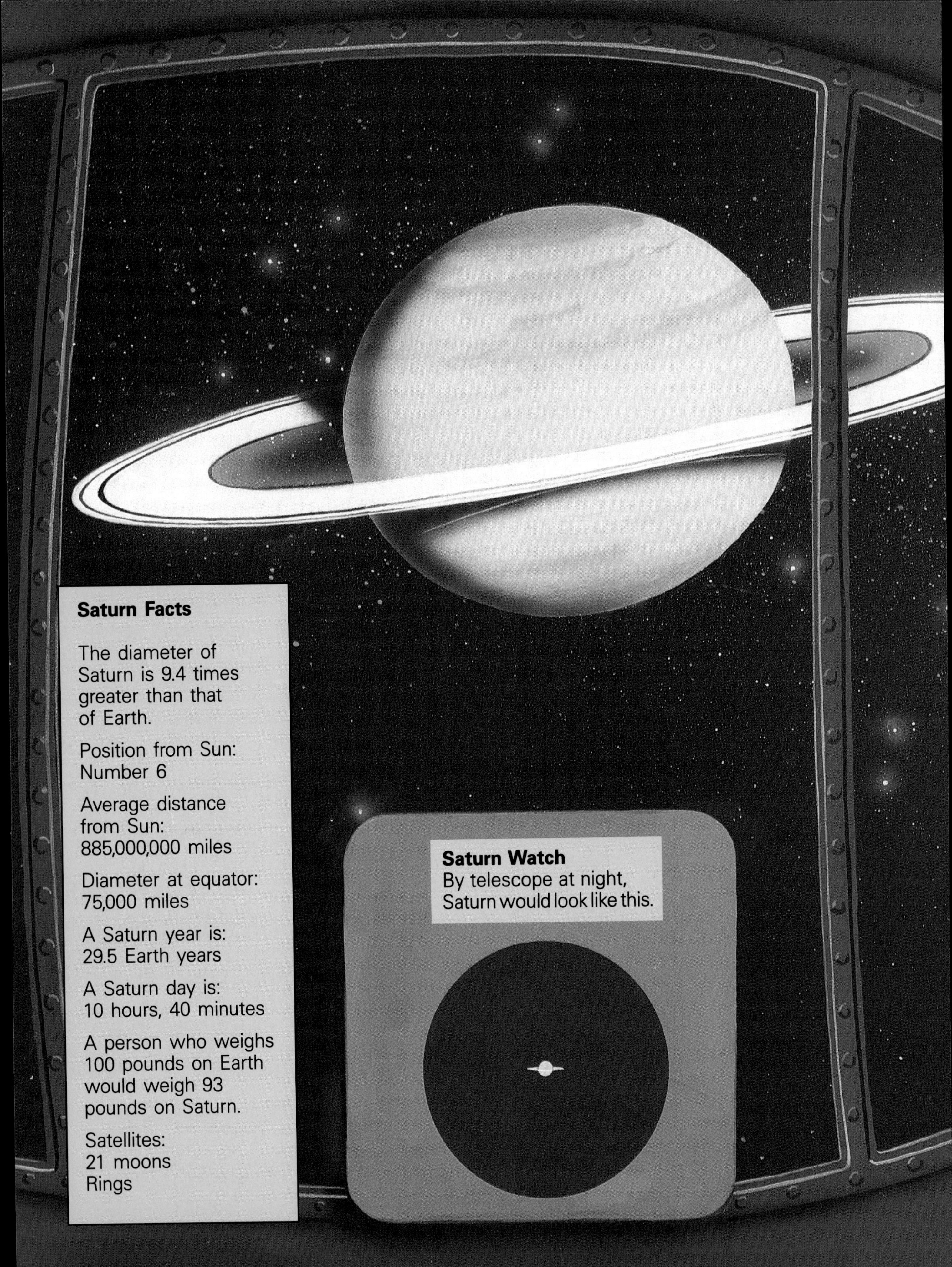

Saturn Facts

The diameter of Saturn is 9.4 times greater than that of Earth.

Position from Sun: Number 6

Average distance from Sun: 885,000,000 miles

Diameter at equator: 75,000 miles

A Saturn year is: 29.5 Earth years

A Saturn day is: 10 hours, 40 minutes

A person who weighs 100 pounds on Earth would weigh 93 pounds on Saturn.

Satellites: 21 moons Rings

Saturn Watch
By telescope at night, Saturn would look like this.

HALL OF SATURN

You are now opposite the planet Saturn. This is what you would have seen if you had been in the Voyager spacecraft that took pictures of Saturn in 1981. Look at the famous rings. To give you some idea of the scale, the rings actually extend 171,000 miles into space, although they're only about half a mile thick. They are made of icy objects – some small, some as big as a house. Gravity holds them in their "track" as they revolve in orbits around the planet.

As you can see, Saturn is yellow-orange. Its atmosphere seems to be composed of swirling gases, like Jupiter's. It's a very big planet (only Jupiter is larger), but it's the least dense planet in our solar system. If you could find a body of water large enough to put Saturn in, it would float.

Because it is so far away from the Sun, it takes Saturn a long time to revolve around the Sun – nearly 30 Earth years. It's very cold on this planet – about -300 degrees F – and the wind blows at about 1,000 miles an hour.

Saturn was named after the Roman god of farming.

Christian Huygens recognized the rings of Saturn in 1656.

Galileo saw them as "horns" in 1609.

TITAN

Saturn seems to be a planet of "mosts." It has the most rings and the most moons—at least twenty-one. Titan, its biggest moon, is the second-largest known moon in our solar system and the only one to have an atmosphere.

THIS WAY TO THE
HALL OF ICY PLANETS

→

HALL OF ICY PLANETS

URANUS
THE SIDEWAYS PLANET

We are now at the outer edges of our solar system, in the neighborhood of the Icy Planets – Uranus, Neptune, and Pluto. We're approaching Uranus as if we're in one of the Voyager spacecraft.

Seeing it this close, you realize that Uranus is a large planet. Notice its dark blue-green color. Uranus is so far from the Sun that it doesn't get much light.

Uranus is lying on its side, compared to Earth. One theory is that something large bumped into the planet and knocked it over. Whatever it was had to be at least as big as Earth to push Uranus over that way. For part of the year, Uranus's north pole faces the Sun. Then its equator faces the Sun. Then its south pole. Then its equator. And so on, as it spins on its axis and travels around the Sun.

Voyager 2 gave scientists a good look at Uranus. It photographed thin rings and fifteen moons circling the planet. One of the moons, Miranda, has long, curving valleys and terraces.

Even if we could get to it, we probably couldn't land on Uranus. Although it seems to have a solid core, the outer half seems to be made up mostly of gases.

Uranus was named after the father of Saturn.

Why do they call Uranus the sideways planet?

34

Uranus Watch
Not easy to see, because it's so far away. On a very clear night it will appear as a blue-green small star.

Uranus' Axial Tilt

THIS WAY TO FOGGY NEPTUNE
→

FOGGY NEPTUNE

If we were actually approaching Neptune
like this, we'd be way out in space, far from
Earth. Neptune is so far away that even the
most powerful telescopes can't tell us much
about it. It's covered by many layers of cloud.
Scientists think Neptune has a core of
metal with gases around it.

Neptune has eight known moons and four
rings. Its largest moon, Triton, is a bit smaller
than our Moon. Triton orbits the planet in
the direction opposite to Neptune's other
moons. It looks like it's going backward!

Neptune Watch
Forget this one, unless you have
a powerful telescope.

Astronomers tried to find out why Uranus sometimes speeded up and sometimes slowed down in its orbit. They thought there had to be another planet beyond Uranus that was pulling on it. That's when they found Neptune, and then Pluto.

Neptune is named after the Roman god of the sea.

Voyager 2 discovered four rings around Neptune on August 24, 1989.

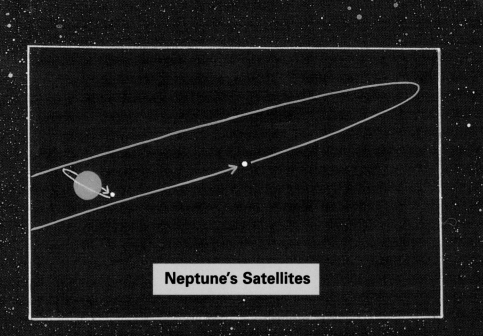

Neptune's Satellites

Neptune Facts

The diameter of Neptune is almost 4 times greater than that of Earth.

Position from Sun: Number 8

Average distance from Sun: 2,790,000,000 miles

Diameter at equator: 30,800 miles

A Neptune year is: 165 Earth years

A Neptune day is: about 18.5 hours

A person who weighs 100 pounds on Earth would weigh 114 pounds on Neptune.

Satellites: 8 moons Rings

THIS WAY TO FARAWAY PLUTO
→

FARAWAY PLUTO

Pluto is the smallest of our nine planets. It is about the size of Neptune's moon Triton. Pluto orbits in an oval path, and its orbit crosses Neptune's. Right now it's inside Neptune's orbit, and it will be there until 1999. So until 1999 Neptune will be the farthest planet from the Sun. Some scientists think Pluto might not be a planet at all. It could be a moon of Neptune that escaped that planet's gravity.

Pluto Watch
Too far away. It's still a planet of mystery.

The name Pluto was chosen because in the Roman myths, Pluto was the brother of Jupiter, Neptune, and Hades —the god of the underworld. Also, the first two letters honor the astronomer Percival Lowell, whose work led to the discovery of Pluto.

Pluto Facts

The diameter of Pluto is about one-sixth that of Earth.

Position from Sun: Number 9

Average distance from Sun: 3,660,000,000 miles

Diameter at equator: 1,620 miles

A Pluto year is: 248 Earth years

A Pluto day is: 6 days, 9 hours

A person who weighs 100 pounds on Earth would weigh 4 pounds on Pluto.

Satellites: 1 known moon

The Sun looks so tiny from here.

You have now finished your tour of the planets. This way to the Dome of Comets and Asteroids.

DOME OF COMETS AND ASTEROIDS

One of the brightest and most famous comets is Halley's comet, named after astronomer Edmund Halley, who correctly predicted where and when it would reappear. Halley's comet appears every 76 years. Its next appearance should be in 2062.

Nucleus

Coma

The core of a large comet is about 10 miles across.

But its tail can stretch for millions of miles!

COMETS

We are in the midst of a rain of comets. Comets are made mostly of ice and rock. They spend much of their lives way beyond the planets, and far away from the Sun. After a while they fall faster and faster toward the center of the solar system. As they get closer to the Sun, they heat up and sprout tails, which always point away from the Sun. One part of each tail is gas. The other part is dust.

Ancient people thought that when they saw a comet, something terrible was about to happen. We know now that isn't true. But it is possible that in a rare instance a comet could fall through Earth's atmosphere, hit the ground, and do damage.

ASTEROIDS

You are now looking at the space between Mars and Jupiter. There are large numbers of objects here that orbit the Sun. They are asteroids. We are in the asteroid belt.

Asteroids are pieces of rock or metal that orbit around the Sun. Some are as small as pebbles. The largest one, Ceres, is a little over 600 miles across.

Try to find Vesta, the bright one. Vesta can sometimes be seen from Earth with the naked eye.

Inside the dome we can get a close look at what the asteroids are doing. Two asteroids have bumped each other, and one of them has been knocked out of the belt. Asteroids that are outside the belt in space are called *planetoids*. Very few planetoids land on Earth. But let's follow these and see where they go.

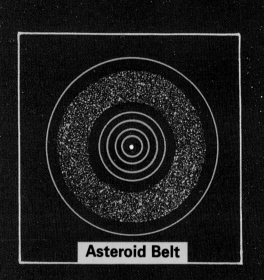

Asteroid Belt

If you drag a magnet over the ground it will pick up some magnetic particles. Some of what you collect will be dust from outer space—asteroid dust!

EXIT TO PLUTO

This one seems to be burning up. It will burn up in the air long before it gets to Earth. It is called a *meteor.*

This one has been attracted by Earth's gravity, fallen into Earth's atmosphere, and struck Earth. Now it is called a *meteorite.*

The Quadrantid meteor showers happen about January 3, between 12 midnight and 4 A.M. The Perseid showers happen from about August 9 to August 14 during the same hours. Every 33 years there's a super meteor shower. The next one will be in 1998.

A meteor is a "shooting star."

Some times of the year are better than others for seeing shooting stars.

THIS WAY TO THE HALL OF SPACEFLIGHT
→

HALL OF SPACEFLIGHT

Spaceflight begins with a rocket blast. Rockets send spacecraft into space, either in orbit or far from the pull of Earth's gravity. To send people into space and have them return safely in a spacecraft is very complicated. Problems of air pressure, weightlessness, and other factors have to be carefully taken into account.

Here are several different kinds of space vehicles. They have been used to explore in different ways.

Man-made satellites are sent into Earth's orbit to collect information about space, or our planet, or other planets. A satellite that moves out past other planets and gathers information about them is called a *probe*.

In 1962, John Glenn (United States) circled the Earth three times in the spacecraft *Friendship 7*.

Sputnik 1 (Soviet Union, 1957) was the first man-made satellite to be put into orbit. It orbited Earth from 143 to 590 miles high every 90 minutes, collecting data.

In 1965, Alexei Leonov (Soviet Union) took the first space walk, outside a space vehicle like this one.

In 1964, the *Mariner 4* probe (United States) flew past Mars and sent back the first close-up picture of another planet.

In April 1961, Yuri Gagarin (Soviet Union) was the first person to circle the Earth, in the manned spacecraft *Vostok 1*.

Freaky Fact
A rocket launched at the equator gets more "boost for the buck" than a rocket launched somewhere else. Any idea why?

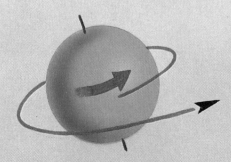

Answer: The Earth spins eastward with greater velocity at 0 degrees latitude—at the equator—than at higher latitudes. The Earth's "spin" can add to the rocket's efficiency.

The first untethered float in space was made by Captain Bruce McCandless from the space shuttle *Challenger* (United States) in 1984.

In 1973, the *Mariner 10* probe (United States) was able to send back the first detailed pictures of the surface of Mercury.

In April 1981, the shuttle *Columbia* (United States) became the first spaceship that could be reused.

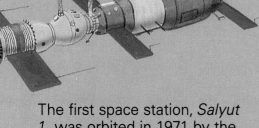

The first space station, *Salyut 1*, was orbited in 1971 by the Soviet Union. Since then, space stations have been much improved.

In 1975, a team of Soviet and American astronauts docked in orbit and spent time with each other.

The Titan booster was used to launch many of the American planetary probes.

On July 20, 1969, two astronauts landed on the Moon in this vehicle. Neil Armstrong became the first person ever to walk on another part of our solar system.

THIS WAY TO
HALL OF THE PAST
→

HALL OF THE PAST

As you walk through this hall, you'll meet some of the people who helped us learn about the solar system.

Ancient people all over the world thought the Sun and stars were gods.

In about 600 B.C.E., Thales (a Greek) said that the Sun and the other stars were not gods. He said that they were balls of fire. He wasn't right, but it was a step forward.

Pythagoras, a Greek mathematician, lived in about 500 B.C.E. He figured out that the world was round.

Anaxagoras was kicked out of Greece in 450 B.C.E. for saying that the Sun was a hot stone that was even larger than Greece.

In about 350 B.C.E., Aristotle came up with the idea that the Earth was the center of the solar system. He said the Earth didn't move, but stayed in one place.

About the same time, the Chinese were saying, "The Earth is constantly in motion, never stopping. But men do not know it. They are like people in a huge boat with the windows closed; the boat moves but those inside feel nothing."

In Egypt in 200 C.E., Claudius Ptolemy realized that the world was round. He said that the planets moved around the Earth like a set of wheels, but the Earth did not move.

Hypatia (375–415 C.E., Greece) was one of the world's first women astronomers.

Nicolas Copernicus (1473–1543, Poland) was the first person to realize that the daily movement of stars could be understood as the effect of the Earth's motion and that planets move around the Sun.

Pythagoras

Thales Aristotle Hypatia

Claudius Ptolemy

Nicolas Copernicus

Galileo Galilei

Anaxagoras

Tycho Brahe

Johannes Kepler

Tycho Brahe (1546–1601, Denmark) began to make records of the movements of stars, planets, and comets. He designed equipment that helped make astronomy more accurate.

Galileo Galilei (1564–1642, Italy) built a telescope with two lenses that made it possible to see an object magnified thirty-two times. Using this new tool, he was able to tell that all the planets didn't orbit Earth.

Johannes Kepler (1571–1630, Germany) established the fact that the orbits of the planets are elliptical and that the planets nearer to the Sun move faster in their orbits than those farther away.

Isaac Newton (1642–1727, England) explained certain things about gravity. He said that the force of gravity between objects depends on their mass and how far they are from each other.

Edmund Halley (1656–1742, England) predicted the path of the comet that now bears his name.

William Herschel (1738–1822, England) discovered the planet Uranus in 1771.

Johann Galle and his assistant Heinrich L. d'Arrest of Germany found Neptune in 1846.

Asaph Hall from the U.S. Naval Observatory discovered the moons of Mars in 1877.

In a famous formula, $E = mc^2$ (energy equals mass times the speed of light squared), Albert Einstein (1879–1955, Germany and United States) described the energy released by stars. E stands for energy, m is mass, and c is the speed of light.

American Clyde Tombaugh discovered Pluto in 1930.

THIS WAY TO THE
HALL OF THE FUTURE
→

Isaac Newton

Edmund Halley

William Herschel

Clyde Tombaugh

Asaph Hall

Johann Galle

Albert Einstein

HALL OF THE FUTURE

Welcome to the twenty-first century! You're at Base 5, a space colony on the Moon. This unique enclosed environment houses about 1,000 people.

Most of Base 5 was built with materials from the Moon—glass made from lunar sand and aluminum mined from rocks. Slag left over from the mining was used on the outside of the buildings to shield people from cosmic radiation.

The colonists get vital oxygen from two sources. Some of the oxygen is supplied to them by space shuttle from Earth. The rest comes from breaking up lunar rock, which releases oxygen and hydrogen. The colonists mix a portion of the oxygen with hydrogen to make water.

There are many factory pods like these attached to the main colony building. The products made here go to Earth. Electronic equipment, for example, and electric power. Astronomy pods conduct research on distant stars and planets. Farm pods grow food for the colony. The recycling pod is one of the most important buildings. Here, waste is processed and reused so the Moon can stay clean and unpolluted.

The colonists make their own 24-hour day and night so that they can live and sleep as they did on Earth. Aluminum mirrors catch the Sun's reflected light, which also provides energy for growing plants. When the mirrors are removed or covered, "night" falls.

Inside Base 5, there are mountains, valleys, lakes, animals, and plants. Scientists have created many of the features of Earth, but Base 5 seems to enjoy the best of both planets. For example, the colonists have taken advantage of the Moon's lighter pull of gravity. Biking is easier here. so is skiing. And gymnastics are terrific! Instead of driving, people travel this way.

The colonists will continue to explore the solar system. They will make ships to travel to the asteroids and beyond to the outer planets.

Can I try it?

My turn!

EXIT
→
THANK YOU
FOR VISITING
THE PLANETARIUM

Index

About the Contributors

Barbara Brenner, the author, is a writer, editor, teacher, and consultant on educational projects. Most recently, she has been senior editor in the Publications Division of the Bank Street College of Education. Ms. Brenner has written more than fifty books for children, including many on natural science for which she has won numerous awards. She has five times received the Outstanding Science Book award given by the National Science Teachers Association and the Children's Book Council. One of her books, *On the Frontier with Mr. Audubon,* was selected by *School Library Journal* as "The Best of the Best" among the books published for children over twenty-six publishing seasons.

Ron Miller, the illustrator, is a graduate of the Columbus College of Art and Design. From 1973 to 1977 he was art director for the Albert Einstein Planetarium at the National Air and Space Museum in Washington, D.C. He is also a founding member of the International Association of Astronomical Artists.

Mr. Miller has won many awards for his books, including Outstanding Science Book, given for *Stars and Planets* by the National Science Teachers Association and the Children's Book Council. He was also nominated for a Hugo Award for Best Nonfiction for *The Grand Tour,* which he coauthored with W. K. Hartmann. Most recently, he designed a ten-stamp set of commemorative U.S. postage stamps (science exploration series).

Dr. William R. Alschuler, the science consultant, has a background in hard science, science education, and engineering, including a Ph.D. in astronomy and extensive teaching experience in the sciences and energy conservation at the university level. Dr. Alschuler is also the founder and principal of Future Museums, a museum consulting firm for museums and exhibits that have science and technological content or are in related fields. He is the author of published scientific studies in astronomy.